THE LONG ROAD TO
HOLLYWOOD

THE LONG ROAD TO
HOLLYWOOD

Shooting for the Stars

JUDITH TWINE BRINN

KP PUBLISHING COMPANY

Copyright 2020 by Judith Brinn
The Long Road to Hollywood: Shooting for the Stars

All rights reserved. In accordance with the U.S. Copyright Act of 1976, the scanning, uploading, and electronic sharing of any part of this book without the permission of the publisher is unlawful piracy and theft of the author's intellectual property. If you would like to use material from this book (other than for review purposes), prior written permission must be obtained by contacting the author at judybrinn1@gmail.com.

Thank you for your support of the author's rights.

ISBN: 978-1-950936-76-2 (Paperback)
ISBN: 978-1-950936-77-9 (Ebook)
Library of Congress Control Number:

Editor: Melanie Polk
Cover Design: Juan Roberts, Creative Lunacy
Interior Design: Jennifer Houle
Literary Director: Sandra Slayton James

Published by:

KP Publishing Company
Publisher of Fiction, Nonfiction & Children's Books
Valencia, CA 91355
www.kp-pub.com

Printed in the United States of America

Disclaimer: This book is memoir. It reflects the author's present recollections of experiences over time. Some names have been changed, to protect the privacy of individuals.

MY FAMILY

DEDICATION

This book is dedicated:

To my parents, whose lives were cut short and never saw me in person achieve my goals. I'm grateful for what you instilled in me during my formative years and for spiritually joining me on my journey!

To my two grandmothers, who taught me to be a strong, intelligent, and independent woman of substance.

To my beautiful and bright daughter, astute son-in-law, and two incredibly adorable grandsons who continue to bring me joy and make me a proud, Mumsie!

Last, but certainly not least, to my love, my husband, who has encouraged me to share my story to inspire those who have had the odds stacked against them. Thank you for being my sounding board, best friend, and a wonderful Grandpa to our boys!

CONTENTS

DEDICATION	IX
INTRODUCTION	XIII
SCENE 1	1
SCENE 2	11
SCENE 3	21
SCENE 4	27
SCENE 5	33
SCENE 6	39
SCENE 7	61
SCENE 8	75
TIPS ON SHOOTING FOR THE STARS	79
ACKNOWLEDGMENTS	83
ABOUT THE AUTHOR	85

INTRODUCTION

On a blustery Spring morning, I was born Judith Cecile Price, a Wednesday to be exact, at Highland Park Hospital in Highland Park, Michigan. My parents William and Arlene Price, already had three children awaiting my arrival. My younger sister was born 18 months later.

I was a child who loved to stay close to home; in fact, I cried every day for all of the years I attended the Head Start program and kindergarten. Sometimes my younger sister was allowed to attend with me so I wouldn't cry. I always felt or sensed that I needed to cling to my parents as tight as I could while I could. It was the start of future premonitions to come.

Mom was gorgeous, a glistening brown skin beauty with a black shiny well-coiffed haircut. She was statuesque five-foot-eight and fashion model thin, with a fabulous sense of style. Even with the glass-eye, she had to wear, sustained from a teenage accident, she still had many suitors before marrying my dad.

There are two different versions of how her accident occurred that circulated for years in the family. The first account, according to my maternal grandmother is that she was running while holding a kite, she tripped and the wooden frame impaled her eye. The second, told by another family member is that my mom announced to her mother plans to marry my father, a heated argument ensued; my Mom was hit on the side of her head with a wooden object. Unfortunately, I was never able to verify either version through my mom.

Immediately following graduation from St. Malachy High School in Chicago, Illinois in 1952, my parents wed and she became a homemaker to eventually five children and a husband, as that was the norm back then.

Mom was an extraordinarily talented artist, a gift I was fortunate to inherit. Our playroom was meticulously painted with popular Hanna-Barbera cartoons; Yogi Bear, Huckleberry Hound, Fred Flintstone, Wilma & Betty Flintstone and Barney. Living in the middle of Detroit, Michigan, Tuxedo, in a house my parents rented from his mother, we had a playroom filled with many books and toys and love.

Let's see, there was a three-foot plastic robot named by its creator "Big Lou," then there was the creepy "Patty Play Pal," she looked like the twin girls from the movie "The Shining." Then there was a four-foot Rocking Clown punching bag, and little pairs of red boxing gloves for us to hone our skills. No "coulrophobia" in this family, clowns were welcome! We were far from rich, but we always seem to have what we needed, and or wanted.

Some days we grew bored with the playroom and ventured into other areas of the house for excitement. These excursions were always lead by my two older sisters who were six and seven years my senior.

Introduction

This particular summer day it was decided that we needed to have a kids club meeting. The venue was a section of the attic, to which we climbed into a cubby above one of our bedrooms.

The instructions were to sit only on the wood frame. As we settled in, hotdogs were passed to everyone by my eldest sister. Born under the sign of Taurus, a true creature of comfort, that wood frame was just not going to suffice. Slyly, I slid over onto to the thick, inviting insulation and nestled in. Sitting with my legs crossed comfortably, I began eating my lunch.

My younger sister saw my adjustment and decided to join me. In her attempt to readjust, she pushed down on the padding causing the panel to detach with me on it. Still sitting in a yoga position, with hotdog in hand, I fell through the ceiling, as if it were a trap door.

Luckily, being a resilient five-year-old, I landed safely on the floor, in that very same position. As I checked myself out I heard the harmonic rhapsody of my siblings, as their heads peered from the opening directly above me . . ."ooohhhh, you're gonna get it!" Much to my relief, my parents were just so relieved that I hadn't been injured, that they let me off the hook; however, my older sisters got a stern talking-to.

Early on we were taught to write the alphabet, color within the lines, sing nursery rhymes, listen to music and read fairytales. One nursery rhyme that stood out to me in particular was "Monday's Child." It's supposed to tell a child's character and future from their day of birth.

THE LONG ROAD TO HOLLYWOOD

"Monday's child is fair of face/ Tuesday's child is full of grace/ Wednesday's child is full of woe/ Thursday's child has far to go/ Friday's child is loving and giving/Saturday's child works hard for his living/and the child that is born on the Sabbath day /is bonny and blithe, and good and gay."

Wait . . . What??? (record scratch). According to the Mother Goose poem Monday's Child, babies born on Wednesday are "full of woe." I looked up "woe" in Webster's dictionary and it means "deep suffering from misfortune, affliction, or grief." Great, what a way to send a child out into the world . . . prepare for the worst. Unfortunately, I came to believe, "no truer words had ever been spoken."

My father was an Army veteran. With all his wounds, both inside and out, he returned home from work every evening visibly exhausted, but always receptive of hugs from all of us kids and a kiss for mom. As an assembly line worker at Ford Motor Corporation, he managed the demands of the job, carried the internal trauma from serving in the Korean War, while raising a growing family, he internalized his challenges.

My parents loved each other, and displayed their affection often. Some evenings after dinner they would turn on the "Hi-Fi" stereo and play Frank Sinatra's version of "Strangers in the Night," this was their favorite song. My sisters and I would take turns standing on my father's shoes, dancing with him. My brother would dance with Mom, and we would all switch partners. My dad always finished off the dance session with a tender dance shared with mom.

Introduction

My father was 6'3", thin build, with dark wavy hair and very handsome. He was an only child as a result of a miscarriage his mother suffered one year prior to his birth. He was a very gentle soul who suffered from what is known today as bipolar disorder. There were no known successful treatments in the 50s or 60s, nor had they even given the condition a name. The symptoms of the disease began to surface when he was about ten years old. He was sent to live with his mom's sister, her husband and two cousins on their farm in Kalamazoo, Michigan.

THE LONG ROAD TO
HOLLYWOOD

SCENE 1

Back in the early 50's–60's, Jim Crow laws were in full effect. Teaching jobs, even with credentials were not given to people of color. My paternal grandmother, Georgia, or Granny was of mixed heritage with a lighter skin tone and she was therefore able to pass for white to secure a teaching position at the same rate her white colleagues received. My father's bronze skin tone would not have allowed him to pass for White, so off to the farm he went, feeling rejected, and abandoned. During this time, adding insult to injury, his mother remarried without his prior knowledge, unveiling episodes of depression and manic behavior.

Years later, Granny did the exact same thing to me. After a two-week visit with me at my home in Northern California, we talked and reconnected in a way that I felt we had really strengthened our bond after years apart, only communicating by telephone and through mail.

Approximately one month later I received a card that I thought was a thank you note from her, was instead a wedding announcement. Granny had gotten married.

THE LONG ROAD TO HOLLYWOOD

I was stunned! She never once mentioned this man to me, let alone that she ever planned to marry again. I now know the exact pain my father felt. Lost in my feelings, I never responded, nor did I ever meet him. He died approximately three years later. She never remarried. Some years later, we reunited at my sister's wedding.

Granny was a renaissance woman. She earned a master's degree in education from the University of Michigan in 1945. Granny continued her studies at the University of Michigan and Wayne State University, earning various degrees and certificates. She was an elementary school teacher until she retired. Granny was free to travel during the summer months, including joining us on multiple road trips and her worldly excursions to Europe, China, Hawaii, and other fabulous destinations.

In addition to her education, Granny and her second husband, Grand Daddy Emmanuel, our step-grandfather, owned properties. One of her properties became our family home on Tuxedo Street in Highland Park. We loved going to visit their home, Granny and Grand Daddy owned an apartment building with about 20 units. Since she owned the entire complex, Granny decided to take the whole first floor as their home.

It was a home with two of everything. One side was formal, displaying all her souvenirs and worldly treasures. The other side was more relaxed for everyday living. There was a secret compartment in the basement, a closet stocked with books, construction paper, paint, glue, just everything a young artist would ever need to thrive. My younger sister and I spent many hours in what we called our hideout.

Scene 1

Grand Daddy Emmanuel was a wonderful man. He was tall, dark, and handsome, a true gentleman and an astute businessman. I had no idea about him until much later in life. He always made us feel as though we were incredibly important and truly special to him. He was an excellent chef and taught us the secret of seasoning with sautéed garlic and red onions, which are staples in many of my dishes to this day.

Our life in Detroit was short-lived. Twenty-five days before my sixth birthday, my father went missing. I learned of my father's disappearance from what I overheard being whispered about our home and through telephone conversations my mom had with family members.According to sources, my parents attended an April Fools party at a friend's house; it's my understanding that an argument ensued between my parents, which led to my father abruptly leaving the party. Dad returned home; as we slept, he removed his wedding ring, watch, and wallet, never to be seen alive by any of us again. He didn't even leave a note for us, or that is the way they shared with us.

During the investigation, it was reported that a bus driver stated that my father boarded his bus enroute to Belle Isle in Detroit. While driving over the bridge to the island, he asked the driver to let him off on the bridge. The driver unknowingly was the last person to see my father alive.

Four months later, his body was recovered, and the coroner ruled his death a suicide. A significant void had now engulfed my entire soul. "Wednesday's child is full of woe," played over and over in my mind.

Heartbroken and reeling from the loss of her husband along with the stigma of suicide, my mother moved us to Chicago, Illinois, where we took temporary residence with her eldest sister, Geraldine, Auntie Gerry, to us, and her brood of four boys and one girl. Her youngest son Vincent, only a few years older than I, became my surrogate big brother and favorite cousin. We are still close to this day and vacation together with our spouses as often as possible.

After a few months, Mom relocated us to the suburb of Maywood in Michigan. It was a quaint little town back then, where everyone knew everyone. Maywood was where her mom and older half-sister Maryann resided. We attended Saint James Catholic School with Maryann's children.

As one can imagine, I was too traumatized by Dad's sudden passing. I would cry myself to sleep daily in Sister Mary Josanne's class. She had compassion and took mercy on me, allowing me to rest. Then Mrs. Cronin took over the afternoon classes and was completely opposite of the sister, taping her ruler on my desk persistently, jolting me awake at the start of her class. No one dealt with our grief professionally back then; we just learned to internalize our pain, as our father had done, unsuccessfully.

By the end of the school year, Mom was fed up with her sister Maryann, who instigated several family arguments. Maryann, or Auntie Mae, was pure evil to us. She was jealous of Mom, who was taller, prettier, smarter, and younger than her. Auntie Mae did everything in her power to create discord, including physically attacking mom in the parking lot of the A&P market, where Auntie

Scene 1

Mae worked as a cashier. According to family members, Auntie Mae picked a fight with Mom in the store and followed her out, still yelling at her as she tried to get into her car to leave. Suddenly Auntie Mae starts hitting Mom in the face while trying to gouge out her glass eye. My grandmother and sister intervened.

Shortly after that incident, we found ourselves relocating a second time with a guy's help- a friend Mom knew back in high school. His name was Doc, and he seemed to show up out of nowhere. Expeditiously packing up the house into a U-Haul trailer, we headed West in our blue Ford station wagon. The furniture was delivered once we settled.

The initial plan was to move to Southern California in Los Angeles near my Mom's favorite cousin Carl. Somewhere along our journey, the plan changed. After viewing a beautiful, two-story home in Colorado Springs, Colorado, Mom decided that this was home. I later discovered that Doc accepted a job in Colorado Springs and convinced her to stay.

Finally, it seemed as though paradise was ours. Pikes Peak and the Rocky Mountain range greeted us every morning from the living room's picture window, a huge back yard to play, a house full of pets, with loads of space to grow. There were family outings to discover our new environment and awe-inspiring locations like "Garden of the Gods" in Colorado Springs, pueblos, and even the summit of "Pikes Pike." This move without question seemed to be the perfect decision. Unfortunately, our amazing adventure was tragically cut short after just eight short months.

THE LONG ROAD TO HOLLYWOOD

According to the local newspaper, Mom's "friend" had now become boyfriend/tenant, the Colorado Springs Gazette. Doc became obsessed with her when she decided to end their relationship. On the morning of January 28, 1969, just one month after Christmas and weeks of stalking my mother, he decided if he couldn't have her, no one would.

I believe she sensed something nefarious was in our midst as she stood in the doorway waving to us as we began our walk to school that day. As I continued to walk, I recall looking back, and in the distance, she was still waving.

He entered our home that morning through the attached garage, crept up the stairs to the kitchen, fatally wounding her with a .22 caliber handgun.

As I sat in my second-grade classroom, the door flung open, and one of the office staff handed my teacher a note. Immediately I had a gut feeling that the message was for me. I was rushed from the classroom to the front office, where my sisters and brother were, and they rushed us to the nearby hospital and into the emergency waiting room. We all huddled, holding tightly to one another, as our eldest sister filled us in on the horrific details.

The room was cold, and through my flood of tears, I recall seeing blue-green tiles on the floor and wall, as though we were sitting in a large shower stall. The door opened slowly as the emergency room physician apologetically informed us that our mother passed despite every effort. As we cried and wailed in unison, it was as though I was watching everything unfold from the upper corner of the room, and

Scene 1

it seemed like I had exited my body. I could see myself and my siblings a complete out of body experience due to the shock. It was later reported on the evening news that Dad's body was discovered on Pikes Peak with a self-inflicted, fatal bullet wound.

Instantly, our lives changed dramatically forever. The local newspapers also reported the story. I prayed the following morning before rising out of bed that it was just a nightmare. Unfortunately, that was not the case. The curse of "Wednesday's Child" had struck again. We pulled together as a family, as siblings, now orphans, and wards of the state. My maternal grandmother, Ida Bell, known to our family as "Pretty Mama," arrived the next day and took custody of us. She was aptly given this name by our mom when she was a girl. She was indeed very pretty; caramel brown skin, silky black hair, and more curves than Malibu Canyon. I recall a man in his mid-30's openly flirting with her. The response was priceless . . . "young man, I'm old enough to be your grandmother." As he began groveling, she smirked and strutted away! She was 65 at that time; I had just witnessed the art of flirtation. She loved the name so much that every close family friend and relatives called her "Pretty Mama."

Pretty Mama was a no-nonsense, strong-willed, fearless, independent woman. I proudly admit I get my audaciousness from her. Pretty Mama had just begun her retirement when life threw her an unimaginable curveball, requiring her to now raise five children ranging from age six through fifteen, all while grieving the death of her youngest child. I am forever grateful for all she instilled in me.

Sadly my very first plane ride was returning to Illinois to lay my mother to rest, just as my first limousine ride had been to Saint Cecilia's Church for my father's funeral.

It was 1969; I was in such deep mourning for both of my parents. I felt hollow, empty, as though my heart and soul had been ripped out of my body, creating a void the size of the Grand Canyon. I had no clue of the world events happening outside of our isolated Catholic school environment and suburbia.

Therapy was not highly valued in those days. In the presence of our grandmother, the one session we attended made us all clam-up for fear of appearing ungrateful or retaliated against once Auntie Mae would catch wind of our comments through conversations with Pretty Mama.

We now lived directly across the street from Auntie Mae, her husband, and their three children. Auntie Mae was not very fond of Mom. She displayed her disdain for us daily. Every day, she would tell us that we would never amount to anything. The verbal and physical abuse became the norm. She lined us up and made us sign-over insurance documents that were established for our college education. She used the money to remodel her home and purchase new cars. She would refer to her youngest daughter, who was six years older than my younger sister and me, as "Cinderella," and we were called the "step-sisters." Karma snuck up on Auntie Mae as she watched her husband and two daughters lose their lives to various illnesses. She later lost a limb before succumbing to health issues.

Scene 1

The period with Pretty Mama lasted eight years. After a huge family dispute in 1976, again initiated by Auntie Mae, between Pretty Mama and my sisters, I was forced to make a split-second decision on whether to stay in Maywood or leave to live with our eldest sister in California. Fearful of the threat that we would never be allowed to see my sisters again if I stayed, I chose to start anew in San Francisco with my sisters.

SCENE 2

After three years of living with my sisters, I met and fell in love with my high school sweetheart in 1978. We married in 1980. My new husband, Artie, enlisted in the U.S. Navy immediately after asking me to marry him. Already committed, I felt I would be able to handle military life, but my non-conformist personality began to truly take shape. Becoming a "Stepford Wife" and giving birth every year was not remotely on my to-do list.

In 1977, Sheryon and I met in the 10th grade at South San Francisco High School, and we were instant BFF's. Ken and Ila Wheeler, Sheryon's parents, became my surrogate parents and my one and only child, Monique's Godparents.

I loved being a mom. I poured my heart and soul into trying to make her life the absolute best. I wanted to give her the best I possibly could.

Ken suggested Sheryon and I both take the police department exam; he was already a San Francisco Police Department (SFPD) detective.

The Wheelers were "Godsends" for Monique and me.

I would not have achieved the success I've had if not for all of their love and support. In 1981, hiring women was accelerated and in full motion.

At this point in my life, I wanted a career. My husband was overseas 11 months out of the year. I was a young single mom, except for one month per year. Ken suggested Sheryon and I both take the police department exam; he was already a San Francisco Police Department (SFPD) detective.

On the test day, I forgot my identification. Sheryon and I were seated on opposite sides of the auditorium. She fell asleep during the test from attending a concert the night before. Needless to say, we did not start the academy together. Shortly after me, Sheryon joined the San Francisco Sheriff's department and retired years later as a captain. June 14, 1982, was the first day of training at the academy. All recruits were required to wear court-appropriate attire during the first week of training. Following the first week, hideous gray uniforms were worn until our October graduation, if you weren't "washed out" as they called it. It is my opinion that making women wear dresses during the first week was cruel and unusual punishment.

Everyone was expected to "drop ten" at a moment's notice. That entailed doing ten pushups wherever you stood when ordered. So as you can imagine, anyone standing behind you could get a pervert's look under your skirt or dress if you were told to "drop ten." Our creepy drill sergeant made a point of walking around to take in the view, along with some of our fellow cadets.

Scene 2

Paramilitary training was employed at the academy. Crawling with one ear to the ground, on your side, in the dirt, mud, grass, or whatever the conditions one might encounter during drills was standard. "Cover and Concealment," "Shoot-Don't Shoot," "Control of Conflict," and "Voice Control" were classes taught to toughen up recruits.

Femininity was not allowed during the three grueling months of training. The rules were no makeup, hair off shoulders without the use of hairpins, men's shirts without darts for breasts, men's trousers, belts, and black shoes that had to have a "spit shine" to pass inspection. Mile runs, pull-ups, and standing at attention in the blazing sun until our feet burned were daily routines.

Self-defense instruction included handcuffing, the now rightly banned and potentially deadly carotid restraint. The "Skid Pad" exercise was so much fun as it required trainees to drive on the soap, oil, and water, at a high rate of speed and upon command, turn either left or right, without losing control of the vehicle by counter steering. For me, that was the highlight of the academy. The gun range was one of my least favorite exercises, not because I wasn't good at it, because it was smelly, and painful. Along with learning to shoot handguns we learned to shoot rifles.

We were required to brace the butt of the rifle between our shoulder and cheek. Talk about pain; my shoulder was black and blue from this practice. Fortunately, I wasn't alone in my misery; my two comrades, Mary and Lynette, were severely bruised as well.

THE LONG ROAD TO HOLLYWOOD

We had a week of this training still ahead of us; how were we to survive it?

Following the first day of rifle training, Mary and I met in the bathroom. We applied self-adhesive sanitary napkins to the front of our shoulders that Mary cleverly thought to bring for each of us and concealed it under our jumpsuits. And just like that, we were transformed into sharpshooters! We all advanced to the next level of training.

Boxing was next on the academy training schedule. Opponents were selected by tactical staff. At this point, only four females were remaining out of fourteen originals, which meant I would be paired with one of my friends. Secretly, we agreed not to take it "seriously," however, once we hit the ring, it was no-holds-barred. Lynette and I were paired to fight. Equipped with mouthpieces and boxing gloves, we began our round. Walking around each other, we began sparring little jabs here and there. Out of nowhere, Lynette lands a blow to my abdomen.

Suddenly everything I was taught as a child, wearing those little red boxing gloves, flooded my mind. My stance changed to a defensive one, landing a right punch across her eye. I won the round, but I felt terrible for giving my friend a black eye. After that day, the entire TAC staff called me "Street Fighter Twine." I didn't mind; it was much better than the name our drill sergeant called the three of us; Wiggles, Squiggles, and Giggles, I was Giggles!

At the academy, any display of enjoyment was met with contempt. My drill sergeant promptly informed me that he would make sure the

Scene 2

smile was wiped off my face if I survived the training. Our academy class started with fourteen women, and only four graduated. As my drill sergeant made his way through our line up to shake hands and finally congratulate everyone, I displayed the biggest Cheshire cat smile I could muster; he got the message!

Immediately following the academy, we were thrust into the real world of the "Field Training Program." In this program, you worked every shift with three different "Field Training Officers," also known as FTO. This segment is sink or swim. Everything learned in the academy would now apply. The underbelly of the world was now exposed; death, birth, homelessness, rampant mental illness, abuse of every sort happens, like it or not. I learned many valuable lessons during this time.

I was plucked from my newly assigned station into a special assignment. Back to high school, in various low-income schools throughout the Bay Area of northern California. Initially, I was told any kids swept up in our police sweeps would be rehabilitated without a criminal record. After five years of facilitating drug sales and arrests, I discovered it was all a lie and that the kids were being sent to juvenile detention centers. During this time of undercover work, some friends had no idea I was a cop. As advised, I used my first name but used a different last name.

The premise was to attend different high schools throughout the city, securing three drug buys per person, showing a pattern. Blending in was easy for me, and the students never suspected me as a cop. My "bad girl" persona went over well, leading me to everyone selling narcotics. The only person who knew I was a cop was the Principal. Five other undercover officers were attending the same school; however, we were not allowed to know who for fear that we all could have been exposed if one were discovered.

In a completely different capacity, reliving high school than when I actually attended in the 1970s was an interesting experience. I was asked to be best friends with one of my contacts, attend the prom by two different guys, and chased by a hall monitor for trying to make a drug purchase. I brought my sergeant to the Principal's office, posing as my dad, to not get suspended. It helped my fellow students consider me to be legitimate.

It was easy for me to make buys. I felt bad for the kids selling for their older siblings because of financial situations. I felt good, however, busting adults working throughout the school system selling to kids.

Word traveled throughout the department of my effective undercover skills. I began receiving offers to work with several special units besides narcotics. I did a quick stint with the pawnshop detail, selling books of food stamps to merchants for half the value. They, in turn, redeemed them for full value. I again felt bad for the mom & pop store owners. I turned down vice and arson detail but jumped at the opportunity to work with the Intelligence Unit.

Infiltrating crowds by blending in as an average citizen while assigned to protect President Ronald Reagan and Queen Elizabeth on their visit to San Francisco's Golden Gate Park was thrilling. Again blending in to protect Pope John Paul as he floated down the Mission

Scene 2

Delores Park section of town parade-style in his "Popemobile" and serving as protection in full uniform for his Sunday Service MASS at Candlestick Park are treasured memories. Working in the intelligence detail was the highlight of my policing career.

Throughout my seven-year career with the SFPD, I worked in several different capacities. I did a year in 911 Dispatch, then returned to uniform and was assigned a partner. Along the way, with much hard work, I received numerous captain commendations, yet; I still endured constant micro-aggressions, sexism, and systemic racism to the point of filing complaints and later dealing with the ramifications and backlash.

Around five years into my policing career, I began to stress being a full-time mom, a full-time police officer, and head of household. Artie never supported my career, but I was expected to support his, which I did until I realized I was not being appreciated or honored as a wife should. Enough was enough, my lack of sleep from working the midnight shift, trying to provide a stable home-life for Monique, driving her to and from school, helping her with homework, preparing meals, attending Parent-Teacher conferences, volunteering at her school twice a month, attending birthday parties, and other functions were taking a toll. My plate was full, to say the least.

The cracks were beginning to show in "Superwoman's" everyday existence. Surviving on five hours of sleep daily, I began to slip. On one occasion, I asked my sister to pick up Monique from school so I could sleep. I took a few over the counter sleeping pills. Nothing was working, so I decided to take a few more. I was lost emotionally, flashing back to my father's suicide; I thought maybe he was right to eliminate the pains of trying to deal with everything life threw in his path. The room started spinning, and I knew I was in trouble. Luckily, I was able to call my work partner and tell him that I had taken too many sleeping pills. He called the paramedics and immediately called me back, staying on the phone with me until they arrived. My stomach was pumped, and I was prescribed counseling. My life was seriously out of control.

In my opinion, counseling only is successful if both husband and wife are attending to express their needs from within a marriage. It would not be the case, ghosted again; I was left to deal with my issues myself. That was the beginning of the end of our marriage.

Six years into my career, I knew that I needed to make a crucial decision whether I should stay and advance in rank or live my true passion. I took a year's leave of absence to explore my options. During this time off, I immediately enrolled in an esthetician course at a local beauty college after receiving an offer to work as a makeup artist for a top Bay Area photographer. I humbly declined, knowing I wanted education under my belt before taking any work in the field.

Throughout my years in the SFPD, I had been modeling with different San Francisco agencies adding to my already double life. I was hand-selected out of hundreds to model for the prestigious I. Magnin Department Store in San Francisco's Union Square as an "In House Model."

I loved it! I embraced my true femininity, wearing Haute Couture apparel, designer accessories, glamorous hairstyles, and makeup. I even got my daughter in on the action, appearing in mother-daughter fashion shows on the local morning shows and numerous Bay Area fashion shows and photoshoots.

I particularly enjoyed the makeup process, chatting with the artist on techniques, and discovering any tips they were willing to share. As the year came to a close, and my leave was over, I knew I could never go back to the stressful existence I had been living.

My decision was clear. I marched into my assigned precinct, headed to the typewriter, and executed my letter of resignation. My captain tried his best to talk me out of it, but I had made my decision. Ever the gentleman, my captain, helped me load my car with the contents of my locker, shook my hand, and wished me well. I received many offers to return to the SFPD in a civilian capacity, I humbly declined. "Wednesday's Child" exists no more!

SCENE 3

Leaving the SFPD behind, I had a new sense of freedom. I was ready to take flight with a new career, and I did. Alaska Airlines offered me a position as a Flight Attendant with the top-rated airline. Alaska was very selective and was known as the "crème de la crème" of airlines.

They originally flew only along the West Coast of the United States, from Seattle down to Mexico, and again from Seattle up to Alaska. They added Russia and China in 1991, after the 1989 fall of the Berlin Wall.

Now stationed on the base, Artie was close enough for him to spend weekends at home. Monique was now 11 years old and capable of helping with chores and meal preparation. I allowed my eldest sister to move in with us while dealing with personal issues in her marriage.

The two-month flight attendant training was at the main base in Seattle. It was the first time I had ever been away from Monique for that long. I cried my eyes out the entire hour-long flight, assuring that this would offer us the opportunity for new adventures, cultural experiences, and explorations. Back then, pagers were the most direct way to reach a person, so of course, Monique had a special code that I would promptly answer anytime.

I traveled between Washington and California several times each month. As a flight attendant, you did not work every day, about 20 days per month; however, my status was "on call as a newbie." It meant I literally had a suitcase and uniforms in the trunk of my car, ready to take flight at virtually any minute.

Having a commuter apartment was great; I shared with three of my airline classmates. Everyone was "on-call;" therefore, the chances of everyone being at the apartment at the same time was rare. It allowed me the opportunity to send for Monique and have fun with her in Washington.

There was a lot to do there, and living downtown was exciting. The Pike Street Public Market was within walking distance, as were several great shops and excellent restaurants. My flying route was from Seattle down to Southern California and throughout Mexico. There were, however, several times, I flew from Seattle to Alaska. We flew everywhere in Alaska, including the Arctic Circle. The most exciting trip was to Seattle, Alaska, and onto Russia. Our flight crew stayed in Russia for ten days, flying to different cities, including; Vladivostok, Khabarovsk, and Magadan working the flights.

It was a usual assignment; even flying into Russian airspace, we were followed by two MiG jets, one on each side. Alaska Airlines always lodged the crew in top-rated hotels. However, a particular hotel where presidents and dignitaries stayed was a hotel that was a bit below our standards for people of high rank. The furnishings were dated and drab, and the toilet was cracked and repaired with duct tape.

Briefed about Russian mafia and told to stay clear of anyone driving a Toyota vehicle, as it was their vehicle of choice. Parked outside in the hotel parking lot were KGB operatives watching our every move. A translator and a tour guide showed our flight crew around town. As we walked around with our guide, it became clear that no one there had ever seen a black woman before. Peoples' mouths literally dropped open; a shop owner approached me and rubbed my arm and looked at her hand to see if my color had come off. Another man butchering a pig in the town square offered me the pig's head, for which I coyly shook my head no, but smiling as not to offend.

Our guide took us to the only Chinese restaurant in town. Surprisingly, it was larger on the inside than it looked. There was a band playing to the packed house. As we were seated, a gentleman approached and asked me to dance, just as the band left the stage for a break. He said something to the band and resumed playing, so I danced with him since it was apparently important to him. After dancing with him through several songs, I was able to take a breather as I saw my dinner arrive. He escorted me to my seat and ripped a button off of his shirt, and cupped my hand, depositing the button into my palm. I had absolutely no idea what that meant, then a member from our crew said, "OMG," Judy, you're engaged. Everyone at our table roared with laughter. I still, up to this day, have no idea what it meant.

The following day while touring the town with my crew, a man in a maroon-colored Toyota honked his horn waving erratically. It was my dance partner, and clearly, to me, he was part of the Russian mafia. I clutched onto my comrades and said, "please don't leave my side. I looked over my shoulder for the rest of the trip.

As exciting as this experience felt, there was definitely a fear factor sauntering in the breeze. Ten days without phone contact with family or friends back in the U.S., anything could have happened. I was somewhat relieved to see the agent sitting in his vehicle outside my hotel window.

For all the perks associated with working for the airline, there were just as many burdens, such as furloughs. The normal cycle was after the summer travel rush, September would begin the layoffs of airline employees. Flexibility was a prerequisite, and an ability to think on your feet. I was able to stay employed by transferring from the Seattle base down to Long Beach, California.

I was finally in California; again, a quick 55-minute flight would have me back to the Bay Area. I loved Southern California's energy, but it did have its drawbacks as far as which airport my assigned flight was departing. I chose the central location of Culver City to reside, as there were five airports in which to report within two hours, whereas Seattle only had one, Seattle Tacoma International Airport.

I quickly learned the lay of the land for traveling between airports in Southern California near Los Angeles, LAX, Orange County, Ontario, Burbank, and Long Beach, to work my flights. Eight months

Scene 3

later, after successfully avoiding the furlough, they told me they were transferring me to the new base in Anchorage, Alaska. It was a take-it-or-leave-it situation; now what? Monique was entering high school and was diametrically opposed to becoming a "wilderness girl," so resign I did.

SCENE 4

Getting My Start

Now, living smack dab in the middle of "LaLa Land," I knew it was time to put my skills and esthetician's license to good use in Los Angeles. But where would I start? At that time, I didn't know a single person in the entertainment industry. It was sink or swim, and I was determined to prove wrong the "naysayers," who chuckled and tried to discourage my hopes and aspirations of becoming a Hollywood makeup artist.

As a former Girl Scout, my resourcefulness kicked into overdrive. Every morning I'd hit up the newspaper stand, purchasing industry newspapers such as; the Daily Variety, Hollywood Reporter, along any other trade magazines specializing in casting crews for film or television work. The year was 1992, and looking back, the internet would have made this task a lot faster.

Cold calling for weeks to every casting director listed, I finally spoke to a legitimate agent willing to meet with me and view my work. The company's name alone made my heart race, "Creative Image," . . . how fitting I thought. Even more fitting, the CEO was Tanya Du Shay, a former runway model from Chicago, Illinois.

Upon entering her Hollywood office, portfolio in hand, I had a surge of confidence, turning on my "model on the runway" walk. I knew from one former model to another she would appreciate it, as her assistant escorted me. Beautiful and statuesque, Tanya greeted me with a warm smile and got right to business. As she looked through my portfolio and saw photos of other models and me, she immediately thought I was there to be cast in music videos.

I explained that I had been a former runway model and now was an aesthetician/makeup artist and wanted to work with her agency. During our conversation, she was interrupted by her assistant regarding a critical phone call. She excused herself to take the call in a private room. Upon her return, Tanya asked if I had a professional makeup kit equipped to handle a two-day shoot. I eagerly stated that I did. She said, "great, my makeup artist just canceled, and I'll give you one shot. I'm flying you to San Francisco this weekend to shoot a Keith Sweat & Left Eye music video." That was the start of a wonderful relationship.

Tanya was well connected, and we worked on several successful music videos featuring major artists, including; Boyz II Men, Usher, Shanice, Gerald Levert, and Baby Face, to name a few. One of my favorite music videos was Patti Labelle's "The Right Kind of Lover." Patti's best friend was featured in her video. I, of course, had no idea this was her best bud. He was amiable and easy to chat with, as well as was open to contouring and highlighting. Once he was on the set and everyone was ready to shoot, Patti stopped the production by

Scene 4

standing up and walking over to her friend and said, "I'd like to know who did his makeup?"

OMG, my heart starting racing as I answered from the crowd, "I did!" I hurried nervously to the stage, ready to make any changes or corrections. "What's your name?" Patti asked. "Judy," I answered. "Well, Judy, "Gurl, you beat his face. I have never seen him look so good!" Wow, I was floored and relieved at the same time. I was floating the remainder of the shoot. And of course, Tanya was proud because I was one of her artists.

Tanya and I became very dear friends with a lot in common. We are still friends today. As a matter of fact, we have rekindled our working relationship and are producing and co-hosting amazing podcasts regarding behind the scenes discussions from leading industry professionals. My daughter and Tanya's twin girls have blossomed into beautiful and successful women. The stars were truly aligned in my favor the day we met, being in the right place at the right time. I am deeply grateful she opened the door to my incredible journey.

The world of music videos was still a long road from working in television and film production, which required being invited to join the Local 706 IATSE Makeup Artist and Hairstylist Guild, after fulfilling stringent requirements, then onto making the big bucks. My focus was locked and on tunnel vision!

The year was 1995; the movie, titled "Zooman," starring Louis Gossett Jr., Charles Dutton, and Hill Harper. It was a Showtime original film to be shot on the backlot of Universal Studios. They hired me to be the key makeup artist on my very first film. I was over the moon!

At age fifteen, this is the exact studio that I had visited while on a family vacation with my sisters and I had an epiphany of working in the industry during our guided tour. I wasn't quite sure of what role I would have, as I knew I was too tall at six-feet to work alongside leading men averaging five-feet-eight inches in height, as reported by movie/TV tabloids.

Now, here I am, asked to work on a real television production by my mentor June Josef Sparks. She was a beautiful, seasoned union makeup artist, with whom I was fortunate to work with as her makeup assistant on an American Film Institute student film in 1994. June was only doing the movie as a favor to actor' Phyllis Yvonne Stickney (who portrayed Kizzy in the acclaimed film "Roots") and Charnele Brown, from the hit TV show "A Different World." I officially began my career working on music videos or "mini-movies featuring popular 1990s artists and entertainers.

My heart was racing as I drove through the gates of Universal Studios and parked in the "crew" parking lot. I unloaded my makeup kit from my car and headed to the makeup trailer. People were already busy rushing around, setting things up to meet the scheduled shooting time.

Anxiously, I climbed the stairs, causing a rocking motion to the unsteady trailer as I eagerly proclaimed, "Good Morning!" Instantly, greeted by June, who was doing Lou Gossett's makeup, with a slightly

Scene 4

annoyed look as she remarked, "announce that you are coming on board by saying stepping up!" She smirked and told Lou that I was green, first real production. Lou smiled at me and said, welcome with a twinkle in his eyes. I blushed and immediately set up at my station.

As filming continued, June began to relinquish some of her stars to me for touch up. So when the director yelled "cut," I would run in and powder or "sweat up," Lou, according to the scene. Lou, at this point, had become quite flirty with me. I enjoyed the attention but was still trying to prove myself as a professional.

During a scene where Lou needed to be sweaty, I had to squirt him, so his head and towel were wet. June, who had a crush on Lou, saw him flirting with me, came over and pulled the bottle from my hand, and said, "this is how it's done!" Embarrassed, I watched as she began to spritz Lou; winking at me, he suddenly took the water bottle from June's hand and said, "this is how it's done." June, now slightly embarrassed, says, "Ok, Lou," and marches off. He smiles at me, and I try desperately not to laugh out loud.

The following day on set, Lou invites me to his trailer during lunch break to watch the "dailies." I had no idea what he was talking about, but I was intrigued. Before I knocked on the door to his trailer, I could hear voices coming from inside, so I immediately felt at ease. As I entered, few production team members were inside discussing what had already been shot for the film the day before, hence the name "dailies." Lou offered me lunch as we watched.

Shortly after, everyone exited the trailer, rushing back to set up for the next taping. I got up to head back as well. Lou stood up as though to walk me to the door, pulls me toward him, and kisses me. We kissed again, a longer kiss. Then I pulled away, stating I needed to get to set as well. We hugged and smiled at each other, and I exited the trailer.

Every day was more exciting than the next, openly flirting with me, and I youthfully blushed and giggled. On one occasion, while applying powder to Lou, he leaned in and kissed me on the cheek in front of one of his castmates. The actor laughingly said, "I know someone who's never going to wash her face." Lou quickly replied," I'm never going to wash my lips!" With that, I melted.

We continued our lunchtime rendezvous, teenage type kissing sessions before the producers arrived to review the daily footage in his trailer. We never took it any further, and before I knew it, the film was wrapped, and we went our separate ways. I was on a mission and was not about to be side-tracked. That was my first personal interaction with a celebrity, but not my last. As fate would have it, our team was nominated for an Emmy Award for Best Makeup and Hair Styling. We did not win, but I am proud to this day for being nominated.

SCENE 5

Soul Train

In 1995, I was hired to work alongside my mentor June Joseph Sparks on the Soul Train Music Awards show. I was overjoyed! It was a dream come true. I grew up watching the regular show every afternoon when I lived in Chicago and as a teen in San Francisco every Saturday right after American Bandstand. That's what my friends and I did in high school; I learned the latest dances before hitting the parties, dances, and clubs.

Soul Train was considered a non-union show; however, I could use the hours accrued toward fulfilling my union requirements. It was so fun working on entertainers and singers, many that I always admired, some with whom I worked on their music videos. Initially, I only worked on the show once every three months; then it grew to working every one of their awards shows, Soul Train Music Awards, Lady of Soul, and The Christmas Special.

My career in Hollywood went into overdrive in 1997; not only was I asked to work on the monthly tapings of Soul Train, but I was also asked to be the Key Makeup Artist (second in charge), and by the end of the year, I was promoted to Department Head. It was a spectacular time in my career. Filming live shows at prestigious venues including; The Shrine Auditorium, The Santa Monica Civic Auditorium, The Pasadena Civic Auditorium, Paramount Studios, and press junkets at the Beverly Hills Hotel, it was exhilarating!

Don Cornelius, the creator, producer, and host of the Soul Train television program, introduced me personally to talent that he wanted to receive special attention. As a result, I had the privilege to work on world-renown talents including; the Isley Brothers, Barry White, Destiny's Child, Smokey Robinson, The Whispers, Charlie Wilson, LL Cool J, John Legend, Kenny G, Michael McDonald, Dionne Warwick, Brian McKnight, Boyz to Men, Montel Jordan, The Temptations, and of course the legendary Ms. Aretha Franklin.

Personally escorted to Ms. Franklin's (as she referred herself) dressing room by Don and personally introduced as his top makeup artist, in his iconic baritone voice. Ms. Franklin and I immediately clicked once she discovered my skills and that I was born in Highland Park, Michigan. Being a Michigander herself, she felt a kinship with me.

She began to call me directly instead of having her assistant call me. She would even leave a message on my voice mail if I were on set and couldn't answer. I was blown away to hear the Queen of Soul on my voicemail. One of our appointments was at the Beverly Regency Wilshire Hotel, in the oh so fitting "Pretty Woman" suite, yes from the movie.

She was fun to chat with and was open to makeup suggestions, except for her eyeliner. Her mainstay was Maybelline, black pencil

Scene 5

eyeliner, and she still insisted on the age-old technique of warming it with a match before applying. Through our discussions, she inquired about some of the other personalities I had worked with. As I began to name specific people, she stopped me at Diana Ross. "How was it working with Diana?" "Oh, she was quiet but nice, I replied. "Hmmm, that's interesting," the Queen of Soul replied, with a slight smirk.

A year later, to my surprise, Diahann Carroll would ask me the exact same question about working with Aretha and Diana. It was quite interesting to me that "divas" were each curious about the others. Even more interesting is that Diahann began to call me personally instead of having her assistant call after discovering that Aretha did! It still makes me giggle.

Aretha and I discussed various Motown artists, including Smoky Robinson, who was like a brother to her. They knew each other from childhood. Man, I was on cloud nine as I left her suite and floated even higher when I spied a silhouette of a gentleman walking towards me with a familiar stride in the lobby. As we approached each other and exchanged greetings, I was for once obviously star-struck realizing that man was Sidney Poitier, "be still my beating heart!"

My next encounter with Ms. Franklin was in her suite at the Universal Amphitheater. She was headlining a two-night concert. Again, as I applied her makeup, we chatted more about other celebrities and my personal opinion. Once I finished, she paid me in cash and invited me to stay for a get-together in her suite. Of course, I accepted and found myself enjoying an unimaginable evening with every top name in the "biz," including; Smokey, Tyler Perry, Teena

THE LONG ROAD TO HOLLYWOOD

Marie, and so many of Ms. Franklin's dear friends. The Queen of Soul was definitely gracious!

Through Don, I was introduced to the rapper, The Notorious BIG, and his wife, Faith Evans. I went to the dressing room to do Faith's makeup. She was polite but somewhat incoherent, and she almost slipped off the chair as I did her makeup.

I went to the stage area to apply a little anti-shine to Biggie. As I applied his makeup on the wing of the stage, he looked over my shoulder very pensively, sizing up the audience. He never once smiled; however, he did say thank you when I finished. That same evening he attended the Soul Train after-party at the Peterson Automotive Museum held for talent, staff, crew, and special guests.

I chose to retreat home and gave my ticket away. The next morning I learned that Biggie had been murdered by gunshot as he left the event. In that moment, I realized why both he and Faith's demeanor were what they were; concerned about.

Don was good to his staff and the Soul Train dancer's as well. He provided meals at every taping and event, whether it was a KFC two-piece chicken box or a full spread in the venue's dining room. Everyone came to Soul Train to either get their start or show up out of gratitude to Don. That was obvious at his memorial, after his untimely death. All of the dancers from years past and several celebrities turned out to pay their respects, including; Stevie Wonder, the Whispers, Chaka Kahn, and a host of others who performed or eulogized in his honor.

I worked with Soul Train from 1994-2006. It was a memorable experience and one of the highlights of my career as a makeup artist.

Scene 5

I was allowed to bring my daughter Monique with me to assist, introducing her to the world of entertainment, in case she chose this avenue as her career. I wanted to open doors for her and expedite the process of experiencing Hollywood, hoping to help her avoid any pitfalls. The express lane, if you will.

My experience with Soul Train was a door opener. As a result of my work there, Dick Clark Productions called me to work. Since both shows featured popular musical performers, the clientele overlapped and intertwined. I would encounter celebrities I had worked with on Soul Train during my jobs with Dick Clark Productions, American Bandstand producer. These encounters led to more introductions with various stars and more potential clients.

Along the way, I was also invited out on dates by celebrities on numerous occasions. I accepted an invitation once from an incredible vocalist, who was once part of a trio that rhymes with Malimar. He serenaded me on two different dinner dates, only to discover that he was married. My daughter Monique was interning with his wife's event planning company. Fortunately, it was only two dates, and I squashed it as soon I confirmed with him that it was true.

Another asked me to slip away in the middle of taping to sip champagne in his limo. Of course, I declined because I'm a consummate professional!

SCENE 6

The Evers Family

I met James Van Evers through a talented photographer named Tracy that I freelanced with regularly. Her studio was next door to his. We collaborated on several amazing photoshoots. A few of my favorites to work with were for Sandra Bernhardt and a beautiful up-and-coming contemporary jazz saxophonist named Pamela Williams.

Van would pop-in on our photoshoots to see what was happening and chat with me, carefully observing my skills. I was invited to participate in a photo shoot he was doing for Upscale Magazine. I was quite excited about this shoot, as this would be my very first time seeing my name in print for a photoshoot.

Van Evers was accustomed to seeing his name and his entire family's name in print for news articles and photos. Van's father was Medgar Evers, a notable and courageous civil rights activist in Mississippi, the state's first field secretary for the NAACP, and a World War II veteran who was viscously assassinated in front of his home on June 12, 1963.

The movie "The Ghosts of Mississippi" was the Evers family's story of the quest for justice in the aftermath of Medgar Evers's murder. I was asked to work on the video interviews for the movie because the filming was already underway. I was honored, and I was excited to be up close and personal with each family member.

Myrlie Evers-Williams, Van's mother, was first in my makeup chair. Notable in her own right, she was elegant, eloquent, beautiful, and poised, and she put me at ease immediately. It was fun to chat with her. It was hard to believe that a woman of her stature, former Chairwoman of the NAACP, author, activist, journalist, highly regarded, and an in-demand public speaker could be so down-to-earth and engaging.

Van's sister Reena followed; she was delightful and somewhat shy. So shy that she chose to play a juror in the movie instead of herself. Last was big brother Darrell who portrayed himself in the film.

I was thrilled to discover that Myrlie and I shared the same taste in designers and fashion. She even asked my opinion on her choice of attire. After completing her portion of the video, she hugged me, and Van took a photo of us together. Myrlie said that she looked forward to seeing me again soon; what a thrill.

Shortly after that, Van and I began dating, and he invited me to attend the Image Awards with his family at the Pasadena Civic Auditorium. We sat front row during the awards show and at the banquet dining table afterward. Distinguished celebrities centered around us. It was so thrilling to meet people I had only admired from afar; they were curious about me as well.

Van and I worked on numerous magazine spreads and covers together. We were a great team professionally; however, dating-wise,

Scene 6

I felt a void. While working on a photo shoot I caught off guard when Myrlie brought up the "M" word. I'm not sure if it was a pre-planned conversation but initiated while Van was conveniently out of the room.

Myrlie told me that Van was ready to get married and asked my thoughts on the subject. With a lump in my throat, I exhaled and stated that I had just gotten out of a 13-year marriage and just was not ready to enter that arena any time soon. She nodded her head as though she understood where I was coming from.

Our relationship, both personally and business-wise, fizzled out a few months after "the talk." I had moved on and began working with Fox Sports News as a makeup artist. It was the break I had dreamt about.

Approximately six months later, Van invited me to lunch and commented that we never had closure. I agreed to meet him near Los Angeles in Marina del Rey, at TGI Friday's restaurant to keep it light. We chatted about family members and other friends we had in common. Then out of nowhere, Van announced he was getting married.

Through my amazement, I listened to Van describe how he realized that he was in love with a childhood neighbor and that they had rekindled their relationship. He expressed that he was catching flak from people in the black community because she was white.

In astonishment, I managed to encourage him to move forward and follow his heart because this is what his father stood and died for; equality! I even agreed to do his future bride's hair and makeup as a wedding gift; only he could not tell her we ever dated. I didn't want her to have an issue with what happened in the past. He agreed, and we parted as friends.

I kept my word and arrived promptly to prepare his bride for their big day. Oddly enough, I had no ill feelings about their wedding and meeting the bride. She was friendly and easy-going. As we chatted about the look she wanted, Myrlie entered from the top of the stairs and shouted, "My baby!"

Gliding down the stairs in her flowing "mother-of-the-groom" attire and flashing her luminous smile, she headed towards us. I stepped back so she could embrace her future daughter-in-law; instead, she reached out and wrapped her arms around me in a hug. Taken by surprise, I happily hugged her as well. Myrlie floated off to the wedding area as quickly as she had entered.

We fell out of touch, but I remain grateful for the connections I had made through Van and his family. Yolanda King, daughter of Martin Luther King, Jr., became a client and friend through their connection. I had developed a portfolio full of celebrity photoshoots and magazine covers that exceeded my wildest dreams. I had now begun working regularly for Fox Sports News. Little did I know my life was about to change in ways I had never imagined.

One of the most challenging experiences I endured as a fledgling Makeup Artist was when invited to "Day play" on the show, "Moesha."

An established Makeup Artist, invited me to do Cheryl Lee Ralph's Makeup. Cheryl Lee seemed to be in a tizzy over the upgrades to Brandy's dressing room and parking space. Her dressing room had received upgrades, but she wanted more as well as a prime parking space too. I set up my Makeup station only to find out that she wanted to have her Makeup done while she sat under the hairdryer.

On top of that, she was sitting in a low, folding chair. Due to time restraints, I needed to have her ready in 30 minutes. I felt as if it was a test, or maybe a hazing for the Jr. Artist. I literally grabbed a pillow from her sofa to kneel on the floor and worked with hot air blowing in both of our faces. She was not cooperative, but I managed to get her Makeup applied in the allotted time, and retouch on set. Talking about stressful, but I sucked it up and kept going, and she referred me to other productions afterwards so I knew I had passed the test.

I ran into Van Evers about three months after that, and he had just done a shoot with Cheryl Lee. Since I used to work with him, she asked if I were available. He said she spoke highly of you; I was floored!

My work with Dick Clark Productions was an outstanding opportunity for my career in the entertainment industry; thus, I now had my Union status and was allowed to work on television productions. "The American Music Awards" and "Rockin' New Year's Eve" were productions I worked on for a period of four years. Dick and his wife, Kari, were always present and always welcoming. It warmed my heart that they greeted and chatted with talent and the staff and crew as well.

It was exhilarating to work with performers including; Earth, Wind, & Fire, Diana Ross, Macy Gray, and Quincy Jones. I was flattered that Quincy often came into the makeup room; he would greet meet with a peck on the cheek.

Backstage and behind the scenes was a great place to be and experience the magic. I watched Stevie Wonder warm-up on his piano, Gene Simons—in full Kiss makeup startle me as he popped into to corridor flashing his ultra-long and famous tongue at me.

Seal rescued me from a runaway piece of equipment that I was unaware of as I powdered his face for his performance. Bill Cosby gave me a hug, asked if I was being treated well, and said to let him know if I wasn't, as I applied his makeup. I watched P Diddy greet Lenny Kravitz with a slap across his well-fitted leather pants. I received hugs from Patti Labelle and Mya and watched and congratulated Alicia Keys on her first win for her album.

Those were great times, with fabulous people and amazing performances; Elton John and Eminem performed together. Lady Gaga was carried in on a platter and dressed in a meat dress. J Lo, Carlos Santana, Brittany Spears, and Mariah Carey all performed at different times throughout my years backstage. Still, to this day, it's hard to sit in the audience to watch performances. I feel more comfortable backstage.

MY POLICE OFFICER CAREER

Academy Graduation
(with Mary Dunnigan and Lynette Hogue)

Running five miles for final exam
(with Mary Dunnigan)

Assigned to Ingleside Station, Street Patrol

151st Academy Class 06/14/1982 – 10/08/1982

MY FLIGHT ATTENDANT CAREER

Alaska Airlines Flight Crew

Dinner with Flight Crew & Tour guide at the only Chinese Restaurant in Russia

Flight Attendant

Magadan Russia Street Vendor

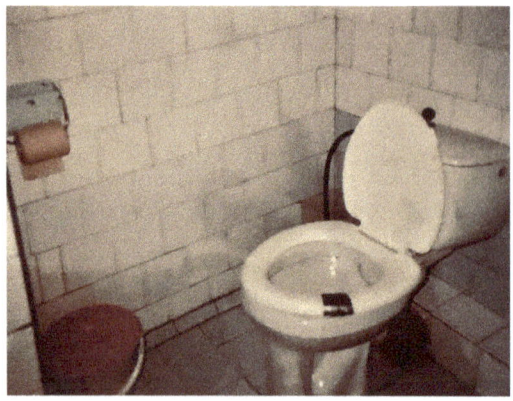

The bathroom in my room at a
Prestigious Hotel in Magadan, Russia

MY MODELING CAREER

MY EMMY NOMINATED CELEBRITY MAKEUP ARTIST CAREER

Headed to the Kodak Theater - to do Makeup for the Academy Awards Show – "Oscars"

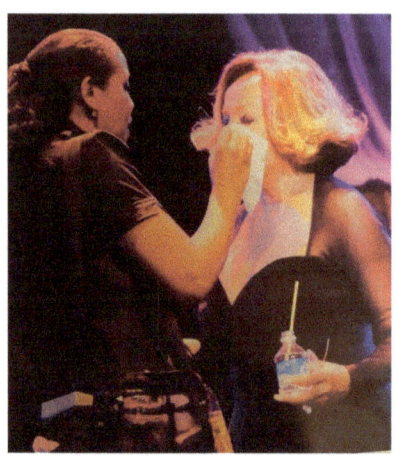

Judy working on Diahann Carroll, Actress, Singer, Model, Activist
(PHOTO CREDIT: LANI GARFIELD)

Credentials to American Music Awards Show, " The Oscars" and the Grammy Awards" For all access production – Makeup

Publicity shot of my company "The A List Makeup Studio"
(PHOTO CREDIT—ROGER MORALES)

Joy Bryant, Actress

Yolanda Denise King,
Eldest daughter of Civil Rights leader,
Dr. Martin Luther King, Jr.

Aretha Franklin, Singer, Songwriter, Actress, Pianist, Civil rights activist
Legendary Don Cornelius, television show host, producer, creator of Soul Train

Judy and Ronnie Lott, former professional football player

Judy and Dave Navarro, Guitarist, Singer, Songwriter, Actor

Judy and Usher, Singer, Songwriter, Dancer

Richard Pryor, Stand-Up comedian, actor, writer

Diahann Carroll, Actress, Singer, Model, Activist
Judy and husband, Michael Brinn

**Myrlie Evers Williams,
American Civil Rights Activist, Journalist**
(Photo credit—Van Evers)

James Earl Jones, Actor of Film, Theater, and Television

Danny Trejo, Actor, Businessman, Activist

Margaret Avery, Actress, Singer

Mario, Singer, Songwriter, Actor

Howard Hewett, Singer

Michael Clarke Duncan, Actor

Pete Rose, former professional baseball player and manager

Actors: Laz Alonso, Keith Robinson, Columbus Short, Chris Brown
Actress: Regina King

Actors: Mike Epps, James Earl Jones, Martin Lawrence, Cedric the Entertainer
Actresses: Margaret Avery, Mo'Nique, Nicole Ari Parker, Joy Bryant

Actors: Victor, Tommy Hollis, Rueben Tate, Charles S. Dutton
Actress: Cynthia Martells

SCENE 7

Fox Sports News

By 1997, I had my foot in the door as what is known in the industry as a "Day Player," meaning I worked on an on-call basis. I "Day Played" on a variety of sitcoms, commercials, and pilots. From my humble beginnings, there I was on the Hollywood set of shows including; Moesha, The Parker's, The Steve Harvey Show, Any Day Now, Inconceivable, Night Stalker, Motown Live, Lou Rawls Parade of Stars, Sparks, Good News, and the "The Oscars," The Grammy Awards, and The Spirit Awards. Nothing was on a daily basis until a little cable show called "Fox Sports News" asked me to become a permanent part of the makeup team.

The premise of the show was sports talk, all day and all night. Mercy! Being raised by "Pretty Mama," we did not watch sports at all. Across the street at Auntie Mae's house, I would see my uncle watching a Cubs game regularly; I found it to be quite boring.

My husband at the time, Artie, was a sports fanatic. Having played basketball, football, and boxing, he would turn two televisions on and more than one radio all at once. To add insult to injury, Super Bowl

Sunday at that time fell on the last weekend in January, which happened to be our wedding anniversary.

I found the whole sports obsession maddening; however, since the studio would pay me union wages to apply makeup and touch up between takes, I could gladly suck it up. Besides, I had prior experience with Artie of tuning it out.

On my first day on the job, I was shown around the studio and stage by a fellow makeup artist. Passing by the stage, the door flies open, and three men walk out, talking amongst themselves about the next segment. The show consisted of news anchors chatting it up with retired professional athletes who were now sports analysts.

As we pass by, Nadine, my guide, greets the men with a simple hi, as she continues to escort me around. The tallest of the men directs his attention to us . . . " Nadine, aren't you going to introduce us to your friend?" With that, he extends his giant-sized hand and says in his deep anchor voice, "Hello, I'm James." Nadine, abruptly interrupting, "James Worthy, this is Judy, our new makeup artist."

My eyes scrolled up his 6'9" frame until we made eye contact. He, obviously giving me his best impression of Billy Dee Williams in "Lady Sings the Blues," intensely gazed into my eyes. As I placed my hand in his, I was galvanized!

The flirtation began instantly. My duties entailed preparing the show's talent by applying makeup, grooming hair, and facial hair. Every day James would make it a point to wait until my chair was

Scene 7

empty, even though there were usually two other makeup artists available to do his makeup.

It became quite clear to everyone working the show that James was interested in me and pursuing me. He was whispering flirty comments to me as I touched up his makeup and forgetting (or not caring) that he was still "on mic" and that everyone in the control room could hear his conversation. He seemed unconcerned that while slipping me notes while seated at the anchor desk, his co-anchors could see him.

I was genuinely flattered but very hesitant to accept his invitation. It became so apparent that fellow makeup artists began inquiring about if I was going to go out with him. My immediate response was, "He's a pro athlete, and I'm not interested in being another notch on his bedpost!" With that response, they backed off of the inquiries for a while.

On February 27th, staff and talent were called onto the production stage to celebrate the birthday of "Big Game James," as he was affectionately known in the NBA, where he was acknowledged for being named one of the Top 50 players of all time.

Everyone sang and ate a slice of cake. I hurried back to the makeup room to prepare for work. James entered the room and, in a semi-bashful manner, asked, "You're not going to make me eat dinner all by myself on my birthday, are you?"

It was the third invitation he extended to me, so I accepted, considering it was his birthday. However, I knew he did not have to celebrate alone, even if I declined. I accepted and handed him my business card as we exchanged numbers.

Reading my card out loud, he affirmed, "Emmy Nominated, WOW! You're bigger in this business than I thought." Looking up from reading his card, I replied, "I can say the same for you," I smirked, and then we both laughed. That was the beginning of a long, six-year on-and-off romance and true friendship.

James was a very down-to-earth guy, and we had a lot in common. Surprisingly enough, he never sat around watching basketball; he only watched the highlights for his commentary. He loved to golf and treated me with private lessons. We played regularly at Malibu Country Club and any resort where we stayed. Both of us had daughters, I with Monique and his two, Sable and Sierra.

Our children were especially important to us. Christmas and Thanksgiving were at his home since it was much larger than my place, and his older brother, Danny, his wife, and son would visit from Texas.

At my home, we entertained smaller and more intimate birthday parties. I even met his father on a trip to Chapel Hill, North Carolina, James alma mater.

Dating a professional athlete had its pros and cons. The pros were traveling to Laker events or other pro athlete functions, dinners, signings, and high-end resorts. The cons were having people interrupt an intimate dinner to ask for an autograph. On one occasion, on a flight returning from Puerto Rico, a woman spotted James on our plane. I was sitting on the aisle seat, and he was next to me. The

Scene 7

woman threw herself across my lap, actually laying on my lap, panting and almost hyperventilating, asking for his autograph. He replied, "I will give you an autograph if you will kindly get off of my girlfriend. The woman stood up and apologized to me as though she hadn't realized I was even there.

On a trip to Disney World, I had to explain to his daughters, who were eight and ten years old at the time, why people kept bothering their Dad and interrupting us. I understand now why certain restaurants sections have where celebrities and their families can eat in peace.

James and I had many great years together; however, he had a habit of just taking off for a week or two at a time and pop up again as though nothing was wrong with it. I had already had my fill of that with my then ex-husband. I figured what was good for the goose was good for the gander.

I decided to start dating, too, and the Sports Show was my oyster, my smorgasbord if you will. I dated a few pro athletes, but I decided I just wanted a simpler life. James and I are still friends today, and the time we spent together was enchanting.

While working at Fox Sports News, the show had garnered enough attention to move us from the tiny, rundown stages of the Sunset/Gower Studio to the newly constructed studio on the 20th Century Fox lot.

Somehow I knew I would work there and openly expressed my premonition with a dear friend Rick Byrd; as we drove past the Fox lot, I said, "I'm going to work there one day, I can feel it." He replied,

"I do not doubt if you keep moving at the pace you are . . . you will." And proudly, I did!

Politics never crossed my mind as far as my profession was concerned. As the art world and the corporate world are a strange juxtaposition. I learned very quickly that Fox was based on Republican views; lucky me, little Miss Liberal Democrat. Every show had a Republican tone, as well as sexist and racist undertones. Fox hired me in 1997. Political issues and divisions existed in basically all workforce environments, so it was tolerated but not usually appreciated.

Roger Ails as Chairman and CEO and Rupert Murdock as the owner were at Fox's helm, along with surly upper management. I recall doing makeup for both Ails and Murdoch for a promo for a new show that they were announcing. Uncle Rupi, as the crew privately called him, was crotchety like Ebenezer Scrooge. Ails was flirty with every blonde female on set.

I was assigned to work Fox Sports News, The Jim Rome Show, and The Best Damn Sports Show Period. The NFL Show taped on Sunday, well known throughout the makeup and hair department that only Caucasian women were assigned to work on Stage A. On-air talent, James Talmadge Brown (JB), Howie Long, and Terry Bradshaw would occasionally work on a show segment on stage B. Each one on different occasions would suggest that I work on the NFL show. I would reply, "You'll have to request me!" I do know that JB made requests and denied.

There were analysts, hosts, and guests represented from every athletic league; baseball, basketball, hockey, soccer, aquatics, surfers,

Scene 7

sports agents, sports commissioners, volleyball, ice skaters, boxers, and even comedians, and actors, you name the, we had them! It was exciting to meet so many professional athletes at the apex of their careers and a few infamous ones.

It was my experience that the baseball players needed continuously schooling on corporate etiquette and policy. It was as though they believed that the corporate world and the baseball diamond were one and the same. On two different occasions, I experienced being pulled in unexpectedly for a kiss on the lips by baseball players who were definitely married. Of course, my reaction was to push away and let them know that I didn't play that.

Jim Rome was a no-nonsense guy and had received a massive paycheck for his new show on Fox network. During his first week, he walked into the makeup room, climbed onto the makeup chair, as he was maybe about five-feet-five-inches. He would not say a word and looked straight into the mirror. Finally, by the end of the week, I said, "you know Jim, the way I was raised, when someone enters a room, they say hello." As he settled onto the chair, he looked at me and replied, "You're right; hello, Judy!" From that day on, we got along famously. Six months into his show, he said, "You know, Judy, I enjoy our conversations because you don't take my shit, I like that!" We had a good working relationship that I valued.

One afternoon on the Jim Rome set, I walked over to powder Jim, then over to Pete Rose to do the same. They were both seated in low couch-type chairs, I approached Pete, and he quickly placed his hand on my calf and ran it up to my thigh, saying, "Judy, you have such long legs." I pushed his hand away as Jim Rome explodes from his chair, yelling, "Pete, you cannot do that!" Everyone in the control room saw as well. Embarrassed, Pete immediately apologized and stated that it would never happen again, and it didn't. We became friends, excitedly sharing with me the process of his hair transplant, or as he put it, "Crop Rotation." Pete, however, was short-lived at Fox.

Bruce Jenner was another memorable guest on Jim's Show. It was before his second facelift, as documented on his reality show and pre-Caitlyn designation. Now in hindsight, his odd behavior makes complete sense. He stared intensely into the mirror as I applied a little concealer to the darkness under his eyes. He appeared to make faces and asked for more foundation makeup, powder, and eyeliner. I had the feeling then that if he weren't appearing on a sports show, he would have asked for shadow and lashes.

He seemed troubled as he went on set to relive his Olympic win. I initially thought to myself he's just having difficulty keeping up with the Kardashian's, but now I completely understand. It was a short time later that he ultimately transitioned from Bruce to Caitlyn. I give kudos to her for choosing to live her authentic life.

Another interesting guest was also from a reality television show, the star of The Apprentice. Donald Trump and his then-fiancée Melania was memorable. He entered the makeup room, grumbling a hello and shoving a Mac makeup compact into my hands. Melania followed behind him, making a beeline to the mirror, and immediately began primping, even though not scheduled to be on camera. "The Donald," took a seat and began squirming around in his chair. I

Scene 7

opened the compact and advised the orange color did not match his skin tone. He replied, "It's fine Melania bought it for me." Ok, I answered and began applying his makeup. He heard the producers of the show talking in the hallway he began to squirm again, turning his face back and forth. Since time is of the essence for taping, I continued to work around his constant head moving, when my powder brush swiped across his mouth. "Hey honey, watch that brush, I don't know where it's been." I said to him, "you need to sit still so I can finish."

Then he looks in the mirror and says, "This doesn't look right." "Yes, your powder doesn't match your skin tone as I've already mentioned," I said. Melania finally tore herself away from the mirror, walks over to him, dabs her thumb on her tongue and starts rubbing spit on his face like moms do to a little child. He looks in the mirror again and says, "oh that's better!" "Great, you're all set, enjoy," I then directed them to the exit in a hurried manner.

The hairstylist entered the room and said, "He wouldn't let me touch that nest!" We both start laughing hysterically. "Did you hear him," I asked, he called me honey, then said he didn't know where my makeup brush has been, it took every ounce of strength not to say well you're in luck, I just wiped my ass with it!" We laughed to the point of tears! I'm quite sure he heard our laughter as they proceeded to the stage.

Each day we were given a list of the show's guest lineup, however, you never knew what to expect. Mike Tyson was scheduled and sports commentator and former wide receiver, Michael Irvin approached me stating that he knows Mike very well and that he was known to be very unpredictable, and that he would stay close by and act basically as my bodyguard. I was flattered that he was willing to look out for me.

Just as I was warned, Mike's behavior was extremely erratic. He had just gotten his unusual face tattoo and kept trying to stand extremely close to me as I applied a little powder to his face. Thank goodness Michael Irving kept talking to him and wedging himself between us. At one-point Mike grabbed my arm to pull me toward him saying, "Thank you Miss, Thanks so much!" Again Michael distracted him directing him to his seat on the set. Whew, that was an uncomfortable situation, my deepest gratitude to Michael Irving!

There were days when I just had to pinch myself when the door would open to the makeup room and in walks a legend who doesn't really view themselves as such. One such example was Burt Reynolds who walked in and introduced himself to me, chats a while and actually remembers my name as he thanked me before being swept up by the show producers for his interview.

Then there was actors William Shatner, and Dennis Hopper who on each visit to the show would start their own makeup and then ask me to fine tune it, so down to earth. Footballer Ronnie Lott was a pleasure to work with and was the only guy who could make James jealous of our friendship.

Both Sylvester Stallone and Arnold Schwarzenegger enjoyed the makeup process, knowing exactly what they wanted. I was surprised to see that I was as tall as these two Hollywood giants, and they were

Scene 7

sporting man heels, while I had on sensible ballet flats. It always amazes me that leading men in Hollywood are typically not very tall.

In my behind the scenes position, I was privy to who the celebrities really were when not in the spotlight. I saw how they behaved before the cameras were rolling. How they spoke to their assistants, agents, and others in their orbit. I was expected to perform magic to help them look their best.

Working behind the scenes was not always glamorous or even pretty. I concealed black eyes for Ukrainian boxer Wladimir Klitschko and singer Chico DeBarge. I covered cold sores for actors Andy Garcia and Eric Mabius; of Ugly Betty fame. I trimmed ear, nose, and eyebrow hair, and numerous chin hairs. I extracted black and whiteheads, all for the sake of their reputation.

Like talk show host Keith Olbermann, most cleaned up nicely to see him before sitting at the anchor desk was a true transformation from how he arrived. Tom Arnold was a case in point; he always came in an unhinged state of mind, erratic, reeking cigars, and sweaty. Covering his freshly picked scabs was unsettling.

Fox Sports News anchor Lauren Sánchez was intriguing, and for two years, I was her makeup artist and quasi therapist. Her daily escapades kept me entertained as she maneuvered dating in the industry. She was pretty and easy to work with. On one occasion, Lauren came into the makeup room distraught and crying uncontrollably. She had just been informed that she was being "let go" and replaced by a fellow anchor, with whom she was dating. She was due to go on air within the hour. The wardrobe stylist and I pulled her together, cleaned her up, as we gave her a pep talk. Lauren went on air and handled it like a champion. It was the type of cruelty Fox enjoyed dishing out.

As much as I enjoyed my job, the politics at Fox was becoming vicious and relentless. Eventually, I became part of a racial discrimination class-action lawsuit against the corporation. The Hollywood Reporter covered our story. It even made it to local news stations in Los Angeles until Fox attorneys silenced it all. We were all deposed, and a judge decided in our favor.

Of course, a nondisclosure disclaimer as part of the deal, so I must leave it at that. Eight years had come to a close, onward, and upward!

Now that Fox was in my rear-view mirror, and my daughter Monique was in college, I was back on the road to my ultimate destination, free to explore my options. I had raised my status in the Makeup Artist Hairstylist Guild to Journeyman, the highest position in our industry. It meant I could be department head on major motion pictures or television shows.

I was asked to work a television program called "Ugly Betty" along-side revered makeup artist Beverly Jo Pryor, who had many years of experience and accolades under her belt. We had a ball, regardless of the grueling schedule. We endured the lead actress's moodiness and six overly competitive producers, continually running in and out of the makeup trailer, tellingly us to disregard instructions that the last producer had just given. I managed to keep my sanity,

Scene 7

but eventually, I decided to "ease on down the road" to work on a series of films with Beverly Jo and pal Debra Denson.

The world of motion pictures took a lot more dedication, travel, long hours, environmental adjustments, acclimation to various conditions, and culinary offerings. Here is where my flight attendant experience came in handy. I knew how to succinctly pack my personal items and everything I would need to effectively do my job, and I was comfortable navigating the travel arrangements. My dream was now complete. I had successfully managed to realize my goal of working in Hollywood.

The three of us, Beverly Jo, Debra, and I collaborated on several films together, making our journey a real adventure. We worked on films including; Rebound, Roscoe Jenkins, This Christmas, The Janky Promoters, First Sunday, Freedom Writers, Something New, and Fat Albert.

I had arrived! Invitations to celebrities' homes, parties for Gabriel Union, and Magic Johnson, and others were part of the landscape. Such as, personal makeup services for Spike Lee for a press junket, receiving Perrier Jouet Champagne on my birthday from actor Martin Lawrence, joking on the set with actor/rapper Ice Cube about having been, as he called it, "The PoPo," called family by actor James Earl Jones since he too was a Michigander, a neck and shoulder rub from model/actor Tyrese, bear hugs from actor Michael Clarke Duncan, a personal introduction to actor Denzel Washington by Joy Bryant, hanging out in Regina King's trailer after filming. These are experiences that a little girl from Highland Park, Michigan (Wednesday Child) could not have imagined.

Those were the days, and looking back, they came and went in a flash, it seems now. However, there is one chance encounter that reigns supreme overall. Monique and I had gone shopping in Woodland Hills just outside of Los Angeles to a Create & Barrel store for housewarming gifts for her and her hubby's new townhouse. We were standing at the counter when Monique whispered to me, "Mom, that's the lady from the movie "Joy Luck Club," one of her all-time favorite movies. As I finished my transaction, I looked up and said, "Ming?" (Ming-Na Wen). She replied, "Judy," we hug, and I introduced her to Monique, who was star-struck for the first time ever. The look on her face was priceless. It was the day I realized I had actually made it and fulfilled my dreams!

SCENE 8

Present Day

These days I have retired from the Make-Up Union and moved back to the Bay Area in Northern California with my husband of seven years, Michael. I am close to Monique, her hubby, and our two adorable grandsons. Monique never did follow in my footsteps, carving out her exciting career in public relations for a prominent biotech company. I could not be more proud!

Michael Brinn has certainly been a "Godsend" to me. His return to my life came at a perfect time. Through our conversations, we both discovered that we both had a crush on each other since we were ten years old. The universe has a way of telling you who's the one.

On one of our first official dates, Michael began humming, "Strangers in the Night." Riddled with goosebumps, I asked why he was humming that song. He replied, "What song?" I answered, "Strangers in the Night." He said I wasn't aware; it just popped in my head! We both got goosebumps when I told him that was my parent's favorite song. We both knew then that they were giving us their blessings!

I was offered a commercial photoshoot in the mountains above Palm Springs, California, in the rustic area of Idyllwild. I don't drive in the mountains because of my fear of heights, nor do I drive in snow, and it was forecasted. I tried to give the shoot to Beverly Jo or Debra, however, neither were available. So Michael volunteered to not only drive but to be my make up assistant.

The shoot was rigorous in cold, snowy weather, walking up and down hills and valleys, and climbing onto boulders to do touch-ups. Michael handled it like a pro; in-fact, no one knew it was his first time. On the final day of the shoot, it began snowing. I had a premonition that something was going to happen and asked Michael to keep his phone on, where he could hear it as he is notorious for turning it off.

Sure enough, As we began filming, the actor in the scene collapsed.

I thought at first, it was due to the altitude, and then I realized it was much more severe as the executive producer and his assistant tried reviving him unsuccessfully. Everyone began calling 911, but it would take at least 30 minutes. I called Michael and told him to come to the set right away that someone collapsed. At this point, people began crying; the director walked away from the set as though he were in a trance.

As Michael began to descend the hillside, the director began asking Michael about the whereabouts of the crew in a state of panic. Michael paused to answer when I yelled, "What are you doing? He's down here." Everyone began yelling, "Michael, Michael, right here!" As he ran down the hill, he flew out of his jacket and began professional CPR in the pouring rain.

Scene 8

Medical professionals later told us that the actor's heart had stopped, and he would have died had it not been for Michael. The actor awoke from being in a coma for seven days on February 14th, Valentine's Day, to his wife at his bedside. We met with him later, after his full recovery. Had Michael not been available, who's to say if the actor would have survived?

Many other magical events have happened since we've been together, but perhaps I'll save those for my next book. Right now, we are enjoying our grandsons, gardening, and Michael's homemade, gourmet meals. Occasionally, we work in independent films or photoshoots. And since I am still a Licensed Master Aesthetician, I have independent skincare clientele. Who knows what the future holds now that 2020 has ushered in a whirlwind of changes. I have another premonition that the outcome of the changes will be for the best. I'm still hopeful about the road that lies ahead.

TIPS ON SHOOTING FOR THE STARS

For me, it was a long road, but it was a fulfilling journey.

Here are a few tips of advice to those seeking a professional career as a Makeup Artist, or Hairstylist in Hollywood.

- ★ Be specific about the actual type of Makeup that you want to specialize in, as not to waste time. Such as, Beauty Makeup, Body Makeup, Special Effects, Prosthetics, Tattoo design, to name a few.

- ★ There is a difference between Television/Film Makeup, Print/Fashion Runway Makeup, and Broadway Productions. This is important to know when you are seeking an agent, or manager to represent your career.

- ★ You don't necessarily need an agent once you are a member in good standing with IATSE Local 706 Makeup Artist & Hairstylist Guild. However many have one to negotiate contracts.

- ★ Invest in specialty courses like Airbrush, or Wig Creation if you're a Cosmetologist.

- ★ Take private courses from professionals in the Industry, they may offer you work if you are showing promise.

- ★ Also, be advised that once you've been invited to join the **Makeup Artist & Hairstylist Union** you can only do **Makeup**, or **Hairstyling**, you must declare which one you'll be registered as.

- ★ Non-Union shows you are allowed to do either, however you will need to save every paystub for proof of hours worked, because this is how you are invited to join.

- ★ Check out their website for information on how many hours are required, and other requirements. Also, it's a beautiful website with professional photos of magic taking place.

- ★ Put together a professional resume and an online presence to showcase your work. An online portfolio's in high definition is recommended to forward to potential employers.

- ★ Look for work through professional websites with a listing of crew needed for upcoming productions, unless you're lucky enough to have friends to refer you.

- ★ Be professional, and always arrive 10-15 minutes before your call time to set up and ready to work at your given time.

Tips on Shooting for the Stars

★ Clean supplies are a must, as well as a well-stocked kit. Sanitation is king! Dress appropriately for working conditions, be prepared!

★ Know which state you want to work in, as there are different Unions and have different requirements, i.e., California and New York have different requirements.

★ Check with film colleges to work on student films for production hours.

★ Check your attitude at the door and be a team player. A pleasant demeanor will take you far, so "shoot for the stars!"

ACKNOWLEDGMENTS

Kenneth & Ila Wheeler, my surrogate parents who were heaven-sent. Thank you for your guidance, wisdom, stability, and life instruction on being the best parent I could possibly be!

My Village adopted sisters Sheryon, Maureen Wheeler, Gwen, and Sheila Williams, whom I wouldn't have fulfilled my career ambitions without consistent babysitting! I love and appreciate you guys!

June Joseph Sparks and Beverly Jo Pryor, thank you for being the best mentors anyone could ask for!

Vincent and Keith Randale, my dear cousins, who always reached out to me to keep us connected with our Chicago family. I deeply appreciate you both.

Monica Rene Jones, Debora Gant, and Mary Avila, my motivational friends, whose words of inspiration lit the fire inside me to finish my memoir by introductions and referrals, placing me on the right track. Thank you, my dear friends!

ABOUT THE AUTHOR

Judith Twine Brinn is a woman of substance who has experienced the joy of working in several different careers. From a police officer working undercover in the Narcotics Bureau, Intelligence Division, Street Patrol, Fashion model, being a Flight Attendant, and her ultimate profession as an Emmy nominated Hollywood makeup artist. As a highly sought-after celebrity makeup artist, you could find her in film, print, video, and television.

Now adding author to her list of professions, she also produces and is the co-host of a weekly podcast, Beauty Insiders and Influencers.

Judith is the mother of one daughter, Monique, and "Mumsie" to her two adorable grandsons. Judy and her husband, Michael, reside in Northern California.

MY FAMILY

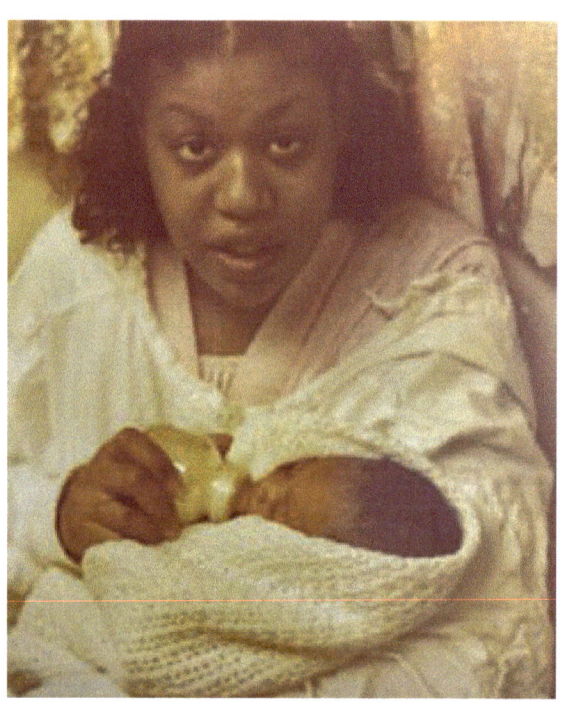

www.ingramcontent.com/pod-product-compliance
Lightning Source LLC
Chambersburg PA
CBHW041325110526
44592CB00021B/2830